THE BOOK OF PITHIES*

Volume II

To Earl,
Best wishes,
Joe Simonetti (?)
1·3·99

Other Books by Joseph R. Simonetta

The Heroes are Us
(A Call to Rescue Our World)

Russell, Alexandra and John
(A Story of Personal and Planetary Change)

The Book of Pithies, Volume I

THE BOOK OF PITHIES*

Volume II

JOSEPH R. SIMONETTA

* a pithy: a brief & forceful expression

GLOBAL
VISIONS
PUBLICATIONS

Copyright © 1995 by Joseph R. Simonetta

All Rights Reserved.

No part of this book may be reproduced or transmitted in any form without permission of the author.

Address inquiries to the author
in care of the publisher.

Published by
Global Visions Publications
2755 Palm Lake Drive
Sarasota, Florida 34234

Book design by Joseph R. Simonetta and Carolyn Willis
Back cover photograph by Ann Simonetta,
July 1994 at Black Canyon of the
Gunnison National Park, Colorado

Printed in the United States of America

ISBN: 0-941594-04-1
Library of Congress Catalog Card Number:
94-96661

*For my closest friend,
my wife,
Ann Kehm Simonetta*

Acknowledgments

Thank you to Dr. Elmer Ruhnke and Dr. Fred Ryersbach for reading the manuscript and for their encouragement. Thank you to Carolyn and Jim Willis of Computer Solutions for preparing the manuscript for publication. A special thank you to Mark Feldstein, for his help, suggestions and encouragement.

Thank you, mostly, to my wife, Ann, for her enduring support and patience, and for acting as a sounding board for the countless Pithies© that have come to my mind.

CONTENTS

UNCOMMON SENSE
1

WE HUMANS
27

TAKING CHARGE
75

LIFE'S JOURNEY
93

Author's Note

Triggered by everyday experiences, these are the kinds of thoughts that occur to us all. I just happen to write them down when they occur to me.

                                                J.R.S.

Uncommon Sense

One cannot make
something from nothing.

Religion must express
the current understanding of
sacredness.

The final outcome of any
endeavor will be colored
by the motives present
at its origin.

We are likely recycled.

We can't teach
what we don't know.

Our bodies house us.

Build sturdy houses.

We are more
than our bodies.

One must experience
both banks of the stream
before one
can know the river.

Religion should unite,
not divide, people.

The future has no patience.

Time is the only survivor.

Remedies help,
criticism hurts.

The only valid generalization
is that generalizations are
generally invalid.

To draw attention to your
faults, find faults in others.

We are mostly victims
of ourselves.

Our problems are found
not in not knowing,
but in not doing.

Remember, you will die.

The past pervades the present.

To love is wise.

We cannot afford enemies.

Patience is more a necessity than a virtue.

Restore what you disturb.

The pessimist sees the glass as half empty, the optimist sees it as half full, and the realist knows it is both.

To serve another
is to serve oneself.

We don't know
what we don't know.

Processes, not individuals,
are indispensable.

Self-interest is an oxymoron.

The rain is as vital
as the sun.

Today is the
mother of tomorrow.

We either all advance
together, or together
we all perish.

Reality endures.

Self-sufficiency is a myth;
we are wholly
connected and dependent.

The ultimate panacea
is knowing there is none.

Truth is constant.
Perception changes.

What we do to our neighbor,
we do to ourselves.

Reality reigns.

Sensitivity can
serve or destroy.

The understandings that we
have, over time, condensed
into concise thoughts will
require gentle and
patient explanation
for others to grasp.

Truth is evident.

When the student progresses,
the teacher graduates.

Simplicity is
not a simple matter.

The wise may not be
so intelligent,
the intelligent not so smart.

Untraceable are the
roots of wisdom.

While knowledge may lead
to arrogance, wisdom surely
results in humility.

Solitude does not
teach sharing.

There cannot be
wisdom without humility.

We are a part of and
apart from everything.

Wisdom costs.

Speak the language
of the listener.

Things are not always what
they appear to be...
but often they are.

We are an infant species.

Wisdom is born through the lens of a keen eye.

The easy way out seldom is.

Thoughts require time to mature.

We are here and now.

Words paint pictures.

Emotion imprisons,
reason liberates.

We can withdraw
only what we deposit.

Those who
make the most babies
get the most votes.

Normal varies.

Age knows youth, but
youth cannot know age.

The prospect of personal gain
distorts our objectivity.

Ignorance is an indefatigable foe.

Youth exits.

Generalizations are the refuge of the uneducated.

Constructive interaction produces progress.

Waste does not
go unpunished.

Yesterday's a fact,
tomorrow's a possibility.

Everyone tells the truth.

God would prefer
that we worship each other.

Vanity is a vulnerability.

Sellers love buyers.

Good friends and good health
are the jewels of life.

Whatever is said
will be repeated.

Smaller bowls, longer chews, leaner meals.

Setbacks are normal.

Life is thick with life.

There is beauty in wisdom.

Our conscience does
not rationalize.

No one can be
with anyone all of the time.

The bliss of ignorance
is shortlived.

Risk is the price
of adventure.

Money can buy health care
but not health.

Every meal is a funeral.

Religion and truth
should be synonymous.

Only those with nothing to
lose can judge impartially.

Killing ends life.

Sex is inevitable.

Simplicity is complexity unwound.

There are no laws higher than nature's.

Advice is best given
when requested.

Everything has limitations.

There's a fine line between
a curse and blessing.

Those who live for approval
stunt their growth.

Hard facts cannot compete
with blind faith.

Competence is not
as easy as it looks.

Common sense
can't be taught.

A judgment is one step
beyond an opinion.

Time is relentless.

Life's about hearts and brains.

Perspective clarifies.

Speak well, listen better.

We Humans

The emotions are not
the womb of logic.

The wealthy and powerful
mine the poor and powerless.

Religions have fragmented
spirituality as nation-states
have humanity.

Truth is veiled.

We are easily influenced.

We learn from each other.

Who we are is a product
of who we've been.

Parents anchor.

Rules require revision.

The extremist seeks dominance, not dialogue.

The wealthy cannot know the trials of the poor, anymore than the healthy can know the suffering of the sick.

Those with food
do not fear hunger.

Uncertainty is unsettling.

We are fallible,
possibly fatally.

Money motivates.

We love to be entertained.

Why such a dearth of common sense?

Passion is mindless.

Scholars love to dissect each other's words.

The heart has a mind
that the brain
knows nothing about.

The wider the perspective
the more proportionate
the response.

To harm another
is to rape your soul.

Unnecessarily loud voices
trumpet insecurity.

We are ill-equipped
for redundancy.

We need to be needed.

Wisdom costs.

People are more interested in
their story than in yours.

Seeds of truth we plant
may blossom at other times
and other places.

The intellect is no match
for the emotions.

The young speak
of graduating,
the old discuss dying.

To know the world's sorrows
is to carry a burden.

We all grow old.

We are prisoners
of our habits.

We never grow tired
of happy endings.

Wisdom is found
in the streets.

People both
fear and delight in change.

Some destroy,
others restore.

The like-minded
fortify each other.

There are many forms
of prostitution.

Too late we learn
what is important.

We all have our beauty marks
and blemishes.

We are so similar
and so different.

We never know
how young we are.

Without incentive
there is no motivation.

Principle can be a
treacherous platform
on which to stand.

Somewhere between order
and disorder exists sanity.

The little things that aren't
supposed to be important
usually are.

There can be no pleasure
in an effort overshadowed
by its outcome.

Too much of anything
doesn't work.

We all need advice.

We do what we do
because we believe
what we believe.

We view others from our
limited perspective, judge
them by our biased criteria.

Words are powerful.

Prodigious are the fruits
of a fertile mind.

Such confusion over power,
profit and progress.

The married seek divorce,
the divorced seek marriage.

There is a great temptation
to indiscriminately judge.

Torture wears many faces.

We all see the
same things differently.

We err.

What is repressed will emerge.

Wrath returns to its origin.

Quality time together
requires quality time apart.

Sympathy imagines,
empathy knows.

The mind is full
of mischief and glory.

There is no sure thing.

Truly great accomplishments
are more likely to be heralded
by the perceivers
than by the achievers.

We are all guilty,
we are all innocent.

We especially like what we like
when it's convenient.

What some find pleasant,
others reject.

Youth cannot comprehend
its foolishness.

Quick responses
are often insecure ones.

The anonymous seek fame,
the famous seek anonymity.

The most mysterious trip
is into another person's life.

There is not always
an alternative.

Trust,
the prelude to friendship,
is a first cousin of love.

We are all inextricably
human.

We exist in cages of our own
making.

What some make best
are excuses.

The morally superior
suffer the morally inferior.

Rare are those both swift of
foot and agile of mind.

The arrogant will
taste humility.

The tyranny of the powerful
results in the anarchy of the
powerless.

There is often no relationship between what should be and what is.

Truth humbles.

We are all insecure.

We fear rejection.

What you do not tell me,
I don't know.

Whatever sells,
will be sold.

Rare is the one
who is not corrupt,
corrupting and/or corruptible.

The boldest statement
can be delivered
in the gentlest question.

The waters of life
teem with sharks.

Truth is riveting.

We are all perfectly fallible.

We fluctuate
between rage and love.

When we're needed,
everyone's our friend.

Redundancy numbs.

The clever exploit
the not so clever.

We are all trying to survive.

We humans are frightfully
self-destructive.

When our credibility vanishes
so does our audience.

We are always trying
to figure us out.

We justify,
rather than resolve,
adversarial relationships.

Where two or more gather there will be disagreement.

We are easily deceived.

The higher we climb the more elite our competition.

An ideal society is something we are capable of defining but not achieving.

The unjust breed turmoil.

Work is something other than
what we'd like to be doing.

Politicians are better
at attacking adversaries than
issues.

That which we want the most
is slowest in coming.

We fish in the thought-streams
of our minds.

The self-righteous
forget their fallibility.

Our beliefs reveal our essence.

Most heroes and heroines
are invisible.

The destitute
are prey for saviors.

A government of
and by the people
may not be for the people.

Our gossip reveals us.

Wealth draws often
undeserved respect.

We are uncomfortable
being judged.

Tampering with one's
self-esteem is tampering
with one's dignity.

While we are programmed
to self-destruct, most of us
accelerate the process.

Creators are unpredictable.

The printed word enjoys
too much credibility.

We so fear letting go
of even that which is harmful.

The information age has
spawned the age of
misinformation.

As we age, we become
more forgiving.

Numbers don't lie,
people lie.

Soldiers are merely targets
for soldiers.

Ignorance is a formidable foe.

We are incapable
of discussing
religious and political
beliefs dispassionately.

Money rules.

We have institutionalized destructive patterns.

When we lie we lose.

We are hardest on ourselves.

Oppression wears many faces.

More people,
more anonymity,
more problems.

Some like the hunt
more than the catch.

Whatever our achievements,
they will be surpassed...
if life persists.

Businesses guarantee
lowest prices through their
doors; religions guarantee
salvation through theirs.

The most insignificant object
can spark the
most brilliant idea.

With life comes scars.

We jump to the defense
of our vices.

The weather changes.

Things taste better
when we're hungry.

Admen are challenged to
transform image
into substance.

Only humans can make liars
out of numbers.

We are uncomfortable
with what is unfamiliar.

We remember those
who remember us.

No one trusts
anyone anymore.

Man's greatest enemy
is ignorance.

Obesity is big business.

Sexual drive is a well-travelled thoroughfare.

Although sometimes tardy, truth eventually arrives.

Liability is the father of responsibility.

The older we get
the faster time passes.

The news is full of old stories
with new names.

Men seek a fling,
women a ring.

Our conscience
is the watchdog of our mind.

Institutions don't fail,
people fail.

We threaten the web of life
of which we are but a strand.

Mistrust is pervasive.

For many there is nothing
sweeter than the sound of
one's own name.

It's comforting to have
a little extra time and
a few extra dollars.

It is we who enable
businesses and religions
to exist, not vice versa.

The more life to which we are
exposed, the more weathered
we become.

We are most agreeable
when our income is dependent
upon our behavior.

If you want to get disgusted
read the newspaper.

We cannot think beyond
our taste buds.

Our minds are unruly.

We covet our addictions.

Our needs blind us
to those of others.

Corruption happens.

The clock moves slowest
when we are most impatient.

Life is a tough game to play.

Small people
can cause big problems.

Death and mayhem
rule the headlines.

Belief systems
vie for recruits.

When you're something
you're something,
when you're nothing
you're nothing.

Our appetites
exceed our restraint.

That which is earned
is more valued.

Without insight
comprehension is limited.

Two can draw opposite
conclusions from
the same observations.

We teach what we are.

Those who vehemently claim
to not care, do care.

Our depravity is depressing.

Those who gush
convey mush.

Some hold on, others let go;
some advance, others retreat.

Small boys are the bane
of small critters.

Our participation is
proportionate
to what we have at stake.

Pain teaches.

Taking Charge

Learn so as to live,
not merely exist.

Our knowledge is
our boundary.

To be disorganized
is to be cursed.

With knowledge,
we discover our ignorance.

Learn to pilot your plane.

Patience is
enlightened self-indulgence.

Self-discipline is
an arduous task.

Trust and honor yourself. ✓

Without challenge
there is no growth.

Learn youth's secret
from children.

Self-doubt weakens our
resolve, inhibits and limits our
potential.

Trust spirit but take action.

Would-be leader
order your own house.

Let patience
be your servant.

Practice being calm.

Selfishness blinds.

Trust what you know about yourself.

You are the only measure of your worth.

Listen to your early-morning mind.

Project, anticipate and plan.

Sharing teaches.

Want less.

You become
what you consume.

Listen to your thoughts.

Recognize the continuity in change.

Want to be
what you are becoming.

Listen. Learn.

Register your thoughts.

We can be only who we are.

✓   Look to today and the future will take care of itself, and the past will become a fond memory.

Remain open.

Spirituality does not suffer
the constraints of religion.

What we desire, we become.

Make some noise
if you want attention.

Repetition teaches.

Take time to be still.

When something is wrong,
change it, don't perpetuate it.

Make time for fun.

Respect your body.

Tenacity pays.

Why suffer what you can change?

Monitor your motives.

Rest is a vital activity.

The mind is the arbiter of stress.

With care, we are durable; we are otherwise vulnerable.

Nothing can compete with perseverance.

Rest must equal activity.

There is no relief
for the compulsive.

One must experience
to know.

Saying is not doing.

There's no payoff
unless there's a pay in.

One who seeks to impress, doesn't.

Seek balance.

Can't can often be can.

We cannot accelerate in neutral gear.

We are our habits.

No amount of exercise
can compensate for
an abusive diet.

Silence is pure.

Take care of the elderly
person you will become.

As we are,
we become.

Think about how you're going
to feel after you've eaten it.

Choose habits judiciously.

Recognize wrong turns.

Mine gems from your thoughts.

Keep promises.

Deafest and blindest
are those
who will not hear or see.

Knowledge is acquired,
wisdom is derived.

Be the best you.

Avoid dead-end streets.

Treat the symptom,
eliminate the cause.

Look below the surface
before diving in.

Get unseated
before you get sated.

Sometimes we need others
to tell us who we are.

A small amount of regular
effort produces large results.

Sharing lightens burdens.

Knowledge is survival.

Chew long,
eat short.

Real men stay sober.

Self care is health care.

LIFE'S JOURNEY

Kindness triumphs.

Let thoughts age.

Motives influence outcomes.

Protect your peace.

Seek solutions not problems.

Teach gently.

Those who fall behind become followers.

We are limited more
by retreating health
than by advancing age.

You can be
brilliant anywhere.

Kindness works.

Let tomorrow be tomorrow.

Nurture rather than abuse.

Question conventionality.

Seldom scream.

Teaching by example is least painful and most effective.

Those who seek predictability will find disappointment.

We can't replicate spontaneity.

We can do what we do because we have done what we have done.

Know other's needs.

Let us not be
trapped by tradition.

Object gracefully.

Showing surpasses telling.

Temper your power
and kindness with wisdom.

Recognize evil.

Those who squeeze every minute out of every hour crush themselves.

We take time for what is essential; we make time for what is important.

We can lose many points and still win the game.

Know when to advance;
know when to retreat.

Let us not become slaves
to our joys.

Objective appraisals
require facts and distance.

Sometimes you
have to take a chance.

That which best warrants
accumulating
is stored in the mind.

Thrills are costly.

We value what we earn.

We must bear the
consequences
of our resistance.

 Know when to keep your mouth shut.

Life is a coin toss alternately coming up heads and tails.

Observation rewards.

Recognize your qualities.

Sound like you know
what you're talking about.

The higher the climb
the narrower the path.

Time is the exchange with
which we purchase our lives.

Weigh the consequences
before releasing the words.

You will always be
the greatest constant
in your world.

Know when to persevere;
know when to let go.

Life requires discrimination.

Often what we say
is less important
than how we say it.

Remember that
your perspective is unique.

Speak less, say more.

The integrity of one's life
will not be the
object of deception.

Time is too precious
to spend too much of it
earning money.

What we do to others,
we do to ourselves.

Our body is our transport.

Know when you are right.
Know when you are wrong.

Looking for the messiah?
Look in the mirror.

Order works.

Replenish before depletion.

The little things that aren't supposed to matter usually do.

Tolerance is eased with understanding.

When present patterns are
failing, introduce alternatives.

Our every moment
impacts our future.

Know which thoughts
to capture.

Make note of
what occurs to you.

People are fragile.
Treat them accordingly.

Resist injustice.

Squeak if you want
to be oiled.

Trust humans least.

Why shout
when a whisper will do?

Our opinion is exactly that.

Knowledge liberates,
pluck enables.

Manage doldrums.

Practice goodness.

Respect real limits.

Suspect and examine fear.

The longest road going somewhere is travelled in less time than the shortest road going nowhere.

Truth can be brutal.

Wisely exceed limits.

Learn to see from
other's perspectives.

Marriage is like a first kiss.
When the time and
circumstances are right,
do it and get on with your life.

Practice kindness.

Rest is a legitimate need.

Take a little longer
and do it right.

Truth should enlighten,
not offend.

With diligence comes
proficiency; with proficiency
comes consistency.

Learn.

Marriage is the stone
that sharpens
interpersonal skills.

Praise not the glory of
distant deities,
but life here and now.

Reveal your love.

Take precautions.

The vessel that you empty,
as you share what you have,
is forever refilled.

Use power wisely.

Without tolerance,
we are lost.

Learning is exposure
and response.

Momentum has power.

Promote laughter.

Reward virtue.

Take responsibility
for the sacred dimension of
your life.

There is comfort in belonging.

Visionaries suffer.

Words exact a dear cost,
weigh them carefully.

Leave no tracks.

Protect your credibility.

Savor joy.
It is a rare treat.

There is never enough time
for over-achievers.

Leave things as you found
them or improve them.

Savor your loved ones.

Let aging beliefs
die a natural death.

Unnecessary resistance
results in
avoidable discomfort.

Mishaps happen.

In our dreams,
we rearrange our past.

We each, in turn,
celebrate and mourn.

To reveal its essence,
an insight must be
chiseled and polished.

Always, we revert
to who we are.

Our only assurance
is insurance.

Beyond exasperation
lies disdain.

Err on the side of caution.

We are each other's opportunities for growth.

Wealth cannot prevent poverty.

Delights taken to excess become chores.

Money is power
but it is not peace.

It is better that we bite our
tongue than eat our words.

Sorrow happens.

Self is the last refuge.

Mortality awakens.

Increased age,
increased caution.

If you seek attention
be a customer.

Experience has
no substitute.

The observant know sooner.

Comfort is an
intermittent state.

Passions vary.

You get what you give.

Naiveté is a
precarious gateway.

Dying is a once in a lifetime
experience.

Anything can be rationalized
but not justified.

Take time to pet the pet.

Wherever we go,
we remain who we are.

With repetition,
that which was novel
becomes ordinary.

Reality can be depressing.

Beyond survival
we seek comfort.

Each moment
is a learning opportunity.

Miracles are exceptionally
good news.

The observant see
what others miss.

Temper your confidence
with competence.

Redundancy zaps
perspective.

Cities harden people.

Eating one's own words
leaves a bad aftertaste.

Sandwiched between birth and
death is this brief
moment we call life.

The meek shall inherit
the muck.

The future is laden
with surprises.

Acquiring money costs time.

There is no hiding
from humanity.

In the recognition of our limits
lies the key
to their expansion.

Lasting peace is found
only in the grave.

As we advance in age,
the child within retreats but
never disappears.

Life passes quickly.
Have some fun.

Most react,
few anticipate.

Small gestures can pay
great dividends.

If you're wrong, back off;
if you're right, persevere.

There are many ways
to say the same thing.

What can't be learned
in the street
can be in a good library.

Birth and death
are the bookends of life.

Compatibility is the product
of compromise

Youth wonders,
age knows.

THE AUTHOR

Mr. Simonetta is a graduate of Harvard Divinity School (Master of Divinity), The University of Colorado (Master of Architecture) and the Pennsylvania State University (B.S. Business). He has been a U.S. Army Artillery Officer, Computer Programmer, Tennis Professional, Entrepreneur, Architectural Designer, Author, Candidate for the U.S. Congress, nominee for the U.S. Presidency, and Founder and Director of PRO EARTH, A nonprofit environmental orgranization. He was born on November 22, 1943, in Bethlehem, Pennsylvania. He wrote these Pithies© in his journals from 1975 to 1995.